Shippo Integration in Angular

A Step-by-Step Guide to Creating

Shipping Functionality

Abdelfattah Ragab

Shippo Integration in Angular

A Step-by-Step Guide to Creating Shipping Functionality

Abdelfattah Ragab

Introduction

Welcome to the book "Shippo Integration in Angular: A Step-by-Step Guide to Creating Shipping Functionality". In this book, I explain how to integrate Shippo into your Angular application.

Shippo is a multi-carrier shipping solution designed to streamline the shipping process for businesses of all sizes.

By integrating shipping into your application, you can create better types of e-commerce applications.

You will learn how to create the labels, calculate shipping costs, and get the fastest, cheapest, and best rates.

By the end of this book, you will be able to enable shipping in your Angular application and handle all kinds of scenarios.

Let us get started.

What is Shippo?

Shippo is a multi-carrier shipping solution designed to streamline the shipping process for businesses of all sizes. It offers a comprehensive API that allows developers to integrate shipping functionalities directly into their applications to efficiently manage shipping logistics.

Create a Shippo account

In order to use Shippo, it is necessary to create a Shippo account first. This account serves as the basis for accessing Shippo's services and functions.

Dashboard Management

The Shippo dashboard provides a user-friendly interface where you can manage your carriers, view shipment history, process returns and access analytics. This centralized management is essential for monitoring your company's shipping activities.

API Keys

Once you have created an account, you will receive unique API keys that are required to integrate Shippo into your application. These keys authenticate your requests and ensure that your application can communicate securely with Shippo's servers.

Test Keys

Shippo offers **test keys** that allow you to simulate transactions without performing real shipments. This is important for developers to make sure their integration works correctly before it goes live.
You get unique API keys for testing that you can use during development.

Live keys

Live keys allow you to authenticate API requests in your production environment.
When you're ready for production, simply replace the test keys with the live keys. That's it, you don't need to change anything else. You don't need to change anything in the code either. Just replace the test API keys with the live keys and you're done.

The Backend

To effectively integrate Shippo into an application, both front-end and back-end components are required. Both play a different role in ensuring secure and efficient shipping processing.

The **front-end** is responsible for the user interface through which customers interact with the shipping system. It provides users with a seamless and intuitive experience that allows them to enter their shipping information and submit transactions easily.
However, the front end alone cannot ensure secure shipping processing. It must communicate with the backend to complete the transaction.
The **backend** is responsible for the more sensitive aspects of shipping processing. It communicates with Shippo's servers using secret API keys that must never be disclosed to the frontend. After the backend has received the response from Shippo, we can save all transaction details in the order object and provide the user with the tracking url of the shipment.

Shippo Process

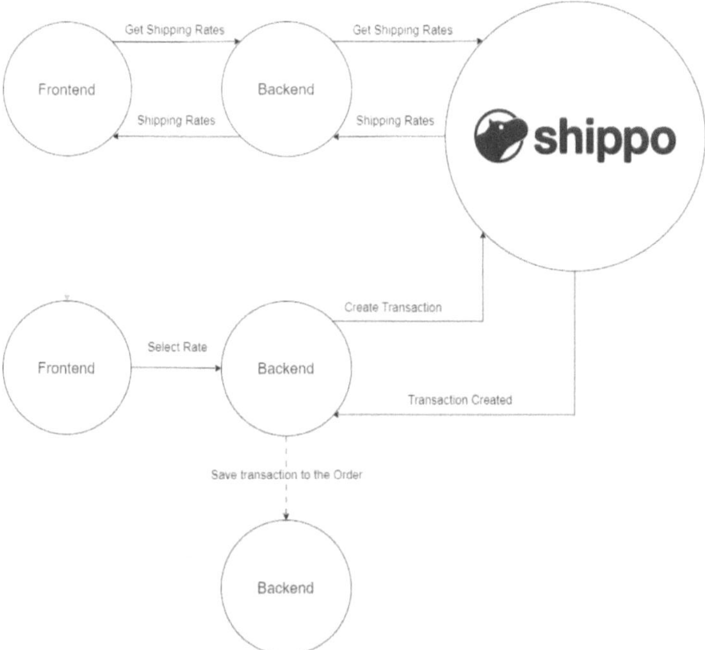

When the user reaches the shipping page, he has already selected the items in the shopping cart and decided to proceed with the purchase.
We have already added items to the cart and are now on the shipping page where the user can select the shipping method.

1. We then send a request to the backend to inquire about the shipping costs for the specified products.

2. The backend sends the information to the Shippo server and asks for the rates.
3. We then return the created shipment to the frontend and display the list of rates for the user to choose from.
4. Once the user selects the rate, he goes to checkout, so we send the cartItems and the selected rate to the backend to make the payment.
5. In the backend, we add the shipping costs to the total amount of the order and wait for the "Payment successful" webhook event.
6. Once we receive the "payment successful" event, we ask the Shippo server to create a transaction for us. We then save the transaction details in the new order. The transaction details include the labelUrl, trackingNumber, trackingUrl and other shipping details.
7. If we save this information in the order record, the user can easily track their shipment at any time later.
This completes the shipping process.

Shippo Dashboard

Shipments are displayed in your Shippo dashboard so that you can manage all business details such as returns etc.

You can manage service providers from the dashboard if you want to add UPS, FedEx and so on. All these details are managed through your Shippo account.

Practical Example

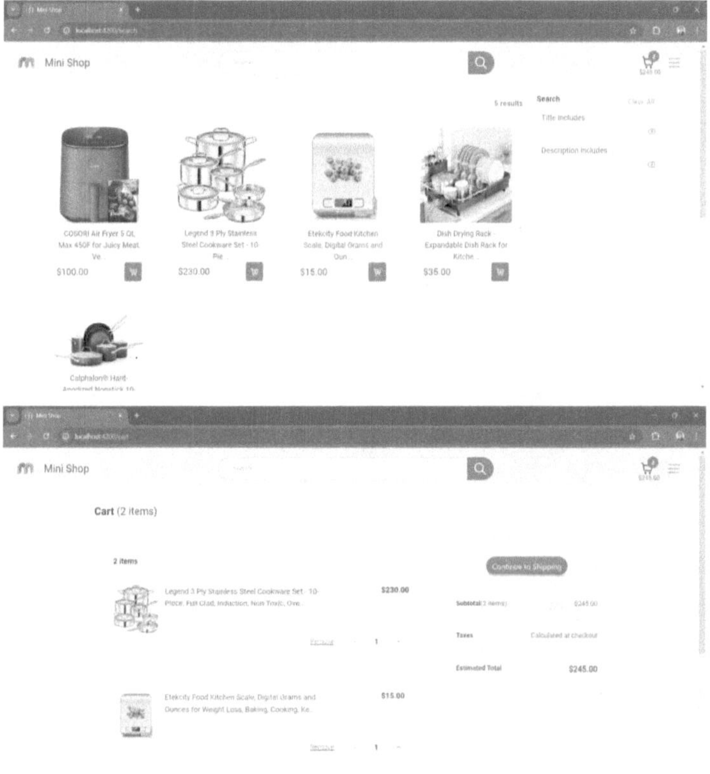

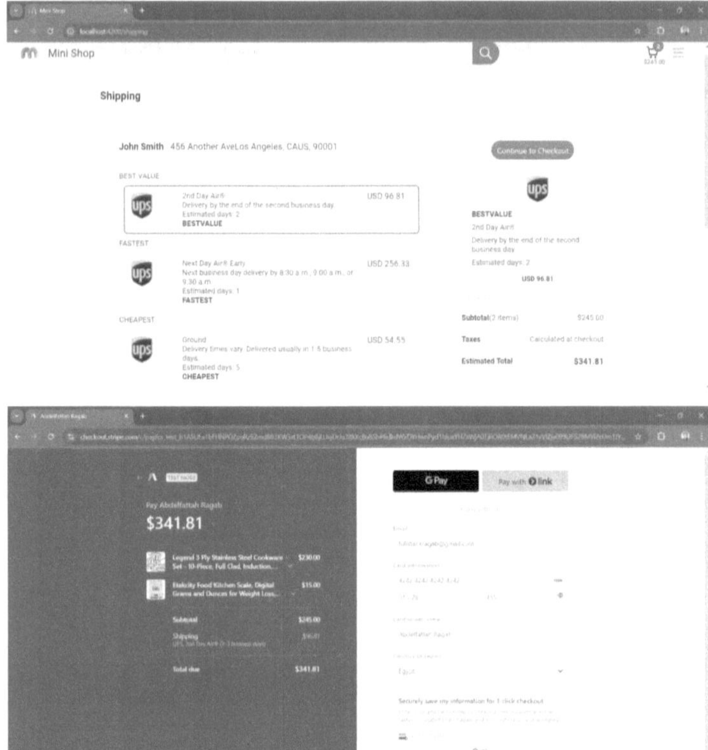

This Angular application consists of three pages, the search page with some products, the shopping cart page and the shipping page. The Stripe form is provided by Stripe, so we do not create it.

On the search page, the products are loaded from the backend.

When you click on the "Proceed to Shipping" button, you will be redirected to the shipping page to select the shipping method.

Once you have selected the shipping method and click on "Proceed to checkout", you will be redirected to Stripe for payment.
Once the payment is successfully completed, the backend is notified and creates a new transaction with all the shipping details saved in the newly created order. The user can later retrieve and track the shipment using the saved transaction information, which includes a tracking number and tracking URL.

Backend

The backend application is created with NestJS.
It has three modules for products, orders and Stripe. We don't connect to the database, we just send an array of products to the frontend.
You can find the code example at
`https://books.abdelfattah-ragab.com`
Download, unzip and run. Don't forget to `npm install`.

The **"Before"** folder contains the projects before we use Shippo.
The **"After"** folder contains the final projects after using Shippo.

You need to install nest cli on your computer.
To start the Nest application: `nest start`
To start the Angular application: `ng serve`

I will start by working on the backend application.

Debug Enabled

In the Nest application, you can start troubleshooting by
clicking on the "Run" menu" → "Start Debugging".
This works because I added a **launch.json** file in the
.vscode folder. It contains the configuration for NestJS
debugging. Simply add this file to any of your NestJS
applications to enable debugging.

Install Dependencies

We need to install Shippo.
```
npm i shippo
```

Shippo Token

Add the shippo token to the **.env** file
```
SHIPPO_TOKEN=shippo_test_9af...
```

Shippo Module

Create a new module for shippo as follows:
```
nest generate module modules/shippo
```

Shippo Service

Create a new service for shippo as follows:
```
nest generate service modules/shippo
```

Export the service in the **shippo.module.ts**
```
import { Module } from '@nestjs/common';
import { ShippoService } from
'./shippo.service';

@Module({
  providers: [ShippoService],
  exports: [ShippoService],
})
export class ShippoModule {}
```

Now we have `ShippoService` **created, let's declare the** `getRates` **method.**
```
import { Injectable } from
'@nestjs/common';
import { Shippo } from 'shippo';
import {
  AddressCreateRequest,
  LabelFileTypeEnum,
  ParcelCreateRequest,
} from 'shippo/models/components';
import { config } from 'dotenv';

config();

const shippo = new Shippo({
```

```typescript
  apiKeyHeader: `${process.env.SHIPPO_TOKEN}`,
});

@Injectable()
export class ShippoService {
  async getRates(
    addressFrom: AddressCreateRequest,
    addressTo: AddressCreateRequest,
    parcels: ParcelCreateRequest[],
  ) {
    const shipment = await shippo.shipments.create({
      addressFrom,
      addressTo,
      parcels,
      async: false,
    });
    return shipment;
  }
}
```

It takes three parameters for `addressFrom`, `addressTo` and `parcels`. It passes these parameters to the shipments.create method and returns the result.

I will declare another method getRate that returns the rate of the specified rate ID.

```typescript
  async getRate(rate: string) {
    return await shippo.rates.get(rate);
  }
```

The last method I will declare here is the `createTransaction` method.

```
  async createTransaction(rate: string)
{
    const transaction = await
shippo.transactions.create({
      rate,
      labelFileType:
LabelFileTypeEnum.Pdf,
      async: false,
    });
    return transaction;
  }
```

It asks shippo to create a transaction based on the specified tariff. The created transaction contains all the details of the shipment. It contains the label URL, the tracking number, the tracking URL and much more.

These three methods are all we need from shippo. We can say that the implementation of shippo is complete. On the next pages, I will explain how to use each of these methods..

Product Dimensions

You will notice that products that need to be shipped must contain information about their size and weight. Here is the product model.

```
export class Product {
```

```
  id?: number;
  title: string;
  description: string;
  imageUrl: string;
  price: number;
  length: number;
  width: number;
  height: number;
  distanceUnit: string;
  weight: number;
  massUnit: string;
}
```

Here you can see what the products look like:

```
private products: Product[] = [
  {
    id: 1,
    title:  'COSORI Air Fryer 5 Qt…',
    description: 'Designed for cooking
novices…',
    price: 100,
    imageUrl:
'https://i.ibb.co/VDGvP3Z/product-1.jpg'
,
    length: 30,
    width: 30,
    height: 40,
    distanceUnit: 'cm',
    weight: 2.5,
    massUnit: 'kg',
  },
```

Get Shipping Rates

In the Products Controller, we create a new endpoint to query the shipping costs for the products in the shopping cart.

We send it an array of items and it will return us an array of rates based on the specified criteria. As you already know, it needs the addressFrom, the addressTo and the parcels.

The addressFrom is our store address. The addressTo is the user address. The array parcels is an array that only contains the dimensions and weight of the products, without any other details.

```
@Get('get-shipping-rates')
async getShippingRates(
  @Query('addressTo') addressTo: string,
  @Query('items') items: string,
) {
  // Our store address
  const addressFrom = {
    name: 'Mini Shop',
    street1: '4727 W 1st St',
    city: 'New York',
    state: 'NY',
    zip: '10005',
    country: 'US',
```

```
    };

    // The user address
    const addressToObj =
JSON.parse(addressTo);
    const parcels = await
this.getParcels(items);
    return
this.shippoService.getRates(addressFrom,
addressToObj, parcels);
  }
```

The `getParcels` method converts the items into parcels by keeping only the dimensions and weight and omitting everything else. You can always check the code to see such small details.

Shipping Page

In the Angular application, create a new page "Shipping":

```
ng g c pages/shipping
```

Add it to the routes array.

Change the button on the shopping cart page to "Continue to shipping" and redirect it to the shipping page.

In the onInit of the shipping page, retrieve the shipping rates and populate the rate list.

Select a Rate

I have placed the featured rates at the top and highlighted them. Once the user selects the rate, I set the selected rate and refresh the interface to display the selected rate and total.

Checkout

The last step after selecting the rate is the checkout. When the user clicks the "Proceed to checkout" button, I submit the shopping cart data and the selected rate to the checkout method.
Stripe is then prompted to create a checkout session and the session id is returned to the front end.

Please read my book "Stripe Integration in Angular" to understand how Stripe works.

The frontend then redirects to the Stripe form, and you can see that the shipping rate is clearly displayed in the checkout form.

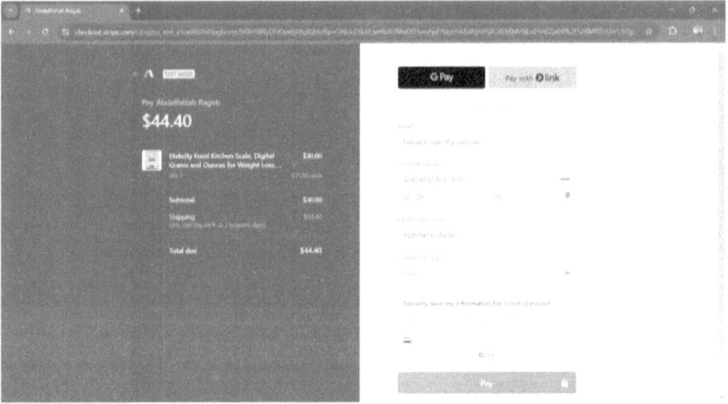

Stripe Charge for Shipping

We set the shipping_options of the checkout session to the selected rate.

```
const session = await
stripe.checkout.sessions.create({
  payment_method_types: ['card'],
  shipping_options: [
    {
      shipping_rate_data: {
        type: 'fixed_amount',
        fixed_amount: {
          amount: preorder.rate.amount *
100,
          currency:
preorder.rate.currency,
        },
        display_name:
          preorder.rate.provider + ', '
+ preorder.rate.servicelevel.name,
        delivery_estimate: {
          minimum: {
            unit: 'business_day',
            value:
preorder.rate.estimatedDays,
          },
          maximum: {
            unit: 'business_day',
            value:
preorder.rate.estimatedDays + 1,
          },
```

```
        },
      },
    },
  ],
  line_items: lineItems,
  mode: 'payment',
  success_url: headers.origin +
'/success',
  cancel_url: headers.origin +
'/cancel',
  metadata: {
    preOrderId: preorder.id,
  },
});
```

Shippo Transaction

Until now we are dealing with rates and we did not create any real shipments yet. Once the payment is completed successfully, we have to create the shipping transaction.

In the payment_intent.succeeded webhook event, we will create the transaction based on the selected rate. Once the transaction is created we then save it to the order.

```
const transObj = await
this.shippoService.createTransaction(
  preOrder.rate.objectId,
);
this.orderService.create({
```

```
  orderDate: new Date(),
  total: preOrder.total,
  userId: preOrder.userId,
  items: preOrder.items,
  paymentIntentId:
paymentIntentObj.paymentIntentId,
  transObjId: transObj.objectId,
  labelUrl: transObj.labelUrl,
  trackingNumber:
transObj.trackingNumber,
  trackingUrl:
transObj.trackingUrlProvider,
});
```

Cycle Completes

This completes the entire shipping cycle. By creating the
transaction, the shipping label has already been ordered
and you should prepare for delivery.
You should save all transaction details for later use, as
we have already done with the order.

Go Live

To go live, replace the test token with the live token.
That is all there is to it. You don't need to make any
further changes. All shipments are now real and will be
delivered to customers.
You can manage carriers, invoicing, returns, etc. via the
dashboard.

Good luck!

Code Samples

Visit `https://books.abdelfattah-ragab.com` to download the code samples.

Conclusion

Congratulations! You have read the book "Shippo Integration in Angular: A Step-by-Step Guide to Creating Shipping Functionality". Now you are able to handle all shipping scenarios with ease. Remember that learning Angular is an ongoing process. Practice makes perfect — create your own projects, experiment with the features you have learned, and delve into the extensive online resources.

Thank you for joining me in my exploration of Angular. I wish you the best of luck on your programming journey. Have fun programming and good luck with your applications!

Media Attributions

Gradient m logo template collection
Image by pikisuperstar on Freepik

Modern annual report magazine page flyer a company catalog
Image by starline on Freepik

Delivery Online Shipping Services online order tracking delivery home and office Courier by truck scooter and bicycle Parcel send to location pins on mobile phone by delivery man
Image by jcomp on Freepik

Don't miss out!

Receive an email when Abdelfattah Ragab publishes a new book. It's free and without obligation.

Also by Abdelfattah Ragab

Stripe Integration in Angular

Stripe is a leading payment processing platform that enables businesses to accept online payments.
By integrating payment processing into your application, you can create all kinds of e-commerce applications.

You will learn how to create the checkout session, how to use webhooks events and finally how to go live. By the end of the book, you will be able to process payments in your Angular application and handle all kinds of scenarios.

Responsive Layouts: Flex, Grid and Multi-Column

Welcome to the book "Responsive Layouts: Flex, Grid and Multi-Column"

In this book I explain the three best-known responsive layouts: the Flexbox, the Grid and the Multi-Column layout.
Flexbox is a one-dimensional layout that only works in one dimension at a time, either horizontally or vertically.
The grid layout is a two-dimensional layout that distributes the elements horizontally and vertically at the same time.
The multi-column layout is a special layout for magazines and newspapers, where the text should flow in columns with spacing, rules, etc.
I'll explain all the properties and their values and how they affect the distribution of elements on the screen.
So let's get started.

Responsive Design

Responsive design is an approach to web design that ensures web pages render well on a variety of devices and screen sizes, from desktop monitors to mobile phones. The primary goal of responsive design is to provide an optimal viewing experience, making it easy for users to read and navigate the site with minimal resizing, panning, and scrolling.

RESPONSIVE
DESIGN

Angular HTTP

In this book, I explain everything you need to know about connecting to backend Rest APIs from your Angular application.
In this book, I will show you how to invoke different methods like GET, POST, and the like, how to use interceptors to inject an authentication token into every outgoing request, and much more.
We will cover all areas of calling Rest APIs with Angular.

By the end of this book, you will be able to call Rest APIs from your Angular application in any scenario. Let us get started.

Angular Shopping Store

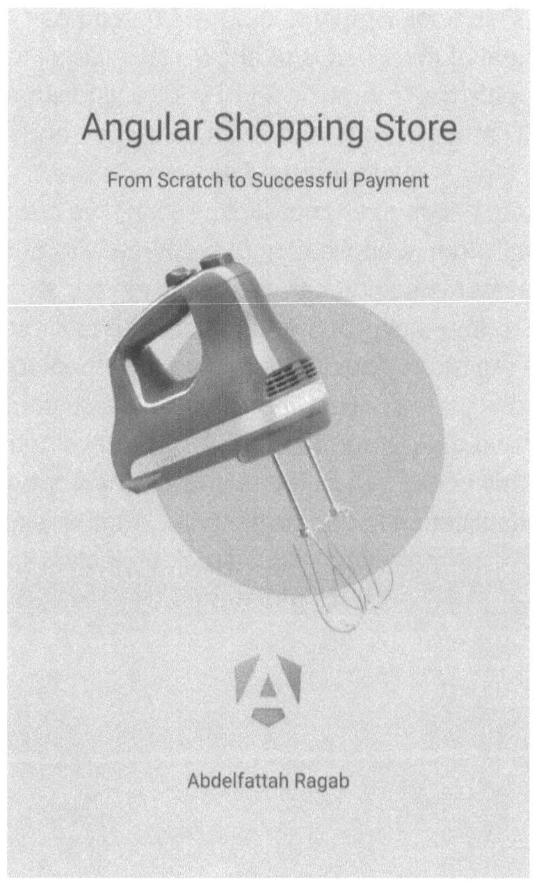

Welcome to the "Angular Shopping Store".

In this book, you'll learn how to create an online shopping store using the Angular framework.
To get your store up and running, you need more than Angular.
You need a backend, a database, payment and shipping gateways and much more.
This book is only about the frontend part.
The goal of this book is to show you in detail how to create the frontend part of your online store.
You will create everything from scratch and end up with a complete frontend shopping store.
To make things even more interesting, I've created a small Nodejs application to help you with Stripe payments so you can sell items in your store.
However, in reality, you need to use webhooks to make sure the money has landed in your Stripe account before you release the product to the customer.
All these details are part of full-stack development.
Also in this book, we will focus only on the front-end part of the application to strengthen your Angular skills and prepare you for full-stack projects.
Let's get started.

Shrova Mall

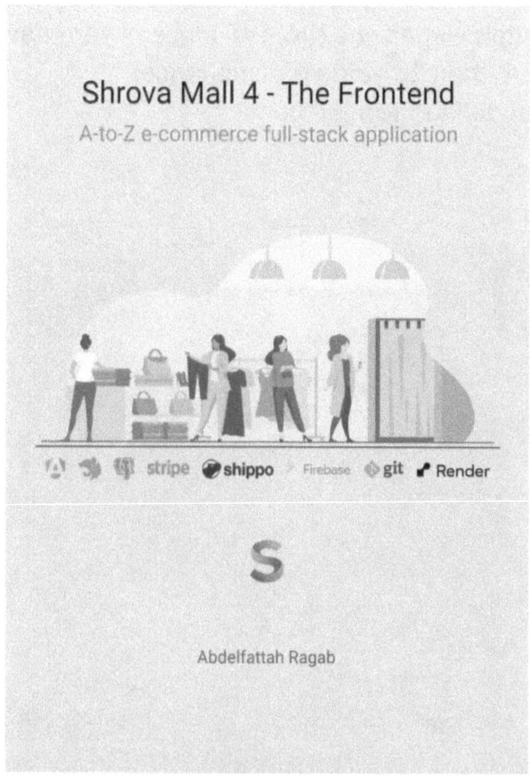

Once you are familiar with Angular, I recommend reading the book "**Shrova Mall**". This is a complete e-commerce solution that allows you to ship products to customers and accept payments online, among other things.

About the Author

Abdelfattah Ragab is a professional software developer with more than 20 years of experience.
https://abdelfattah-ragab.com

About the Publisher

Abdelfattah Ragab is a highly qualified and experienced software developer with over 20 years of experience in the industry. Specializing in front-end development, Abdelfattah Ragab has a deep understanding of Angular, JavaScript, TypeScript, HTML and CSS. Read more at https://abdelfattah-ragab.com